Sunshine

Pupil's Book 4

Erarbeitet von
Inga Bensmann (Weyhe)
Helga Haudeck (Ludwigsburg)
Nadine Kerler (Ulm)
Caroline Schröder (München)

Auf der Grundlage der Ausgabe von
Tanja Beattie
Birgit Hollbrügge
Stefanie Keller
Nadine Kerler
Ulrike Kraaz
Caroline Schröder

Cornelsen

In deinem Buch findest du gelbe Notizzettel mit Symbolen:

Hier erfährst du mehr über die englische Sprache.

Hier erfährst du mehr über Großbritannien.

Hier erfährst du, wie du Medien nutzen kannst.

Manche Aufgaben bearbeitest du zuerst alleine und dann gemeinsam:

Think-Pair-Share

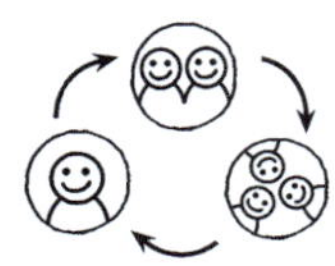

Think: Überlege, wie du die Aufgabe lösen könntest.

Pair: Tausche dich mit einem Partner aus.

Share: Überprüfe die Ergebnisse mit der Gruppe / Klasse.

listen	draw or write	S1 L2 listen to the CD,
talk	play	Track 1 (Schüler-CD)/
read	extra	Track 2 (Lehrer-CD)

Contents

Welcome back

1 Talk about the picture.

2 Read the speech bubbles with a partner.

3 Talk about holidays.
Ask a partner questions.

★ What is in the classroom? Think. Pair. Share.

1 Talk about the pictures.

2 Listen. Point to the pictures. L 13

In picture 1 I can see …

There's … / There are …

3 Read. Talk to a partner. Say: *What do you do in the …? – In the …*

☆ What do you eat for breakfast? Say: *For breakfast, I eat …*

In the morning

I get up.
I have breakfast.
I go to school.

In the afternoon

I do my homework.
I meet my friends.

In the evening

I have dinner.
I go to bed.

4 Talk about Emily's timetable.

5 Listen. What day is it? L 14

On Monday, Emily has Maths, …

After lunch she has Music, …

Time	Monday	Tuesday	Wednesday	Thursday	Friday
9.00-9.30	ASSEMBLY				
9.30-10.30	Maths	Maths	English	Music	Maths
10.30-10.45	PLAY				
10.45-11.45	English	German	Maths	Maths	English
11.45-12.30	LUNCH				
12.30-1.15	QUIET				
1.15-2.15	Music	Computers	Science	English	Art
2.15-3.15	German	P.E.	P.E.	Art	Computers

Note

In Großbritannien beginnt der Schultag mit einer großen Versammlung. Diese nennt man *assembly*.

A trip to London

1 Talk about the map.

There's … / There are …

I can see …

2 Listen to your teacher. Find the sights on the map. Say: *Number 1 is …*

Read the texts.

1 **Tower Bridge** is a very famous bridge. It can open for big ships in about 90 seconds.

2 **London Zoo** is one of the oldest zoos in the world. You can see about 750 different kinds of animals there.

3 **Buckingham Palace** is the Queen's London home. On top of Buckingham Palace you can see the Union flag.

4 **Big Ben** is the name of a bell. The bell is inside the clock tower of Westminster Palace.

Note

The London underground is called the 'Tube'.

Note

Find out more about the Tower of London (8) and Trafalgar Square (9).

L 18 **3** Look at the map. Listen and find the way.

Listen again. Where and when do they go? How do they get there?

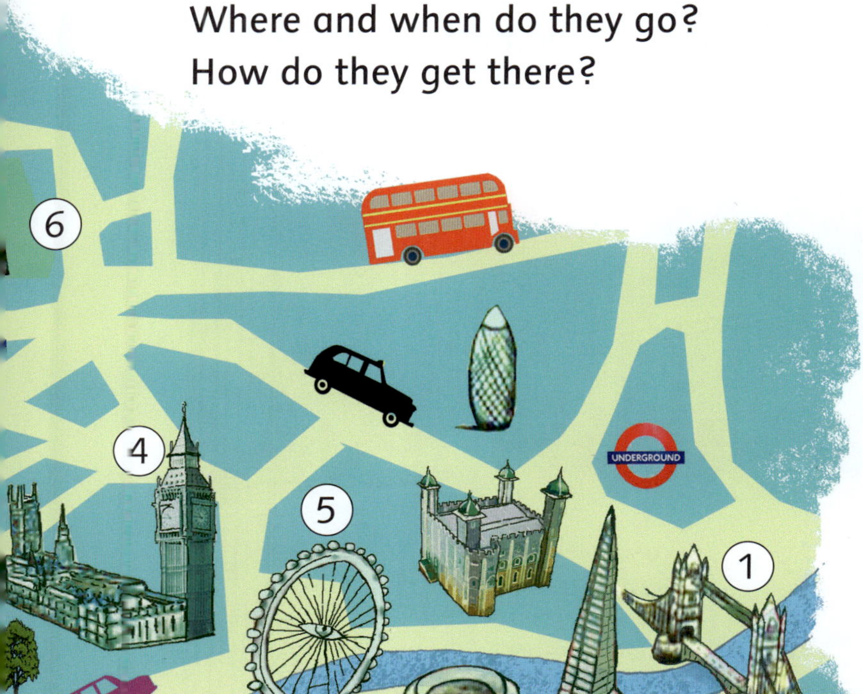

(5) The **London Eye** is a big wheel. It is very high.

(6) **Madame Tussauds** is a famous wax museum. You can see film stars, sports stars, pop stars and the Royal Family there.

(7) At the **Natural History Museum** there is a big dinosaur.

Let's talk

4 Read the dialogue. Talk to a partner.

More: Make up your own dialogue.

Note

It is best to use a card on London transport. Find out more on the Internet. What types of tickets and transport are there? Type in: "London transport best ticket".

1 Talk about the pictures.

There's … / I can see …

2 Read the postcards. Which picture is it?

3 Who is in London? What can you see from the top of the London Eye? What is Harry's grandmother's name?

1

2

3

Hello Jack,

I'm in London with Kate. It's super! Today is my birthday. We are on a boat trip on the River Thames to the London Eye.
You can see Buckingham Palace from the top of the London Eye.

Harry

Dear Grandma,

How are you? I'm in London with my friend Kate. London is great. I like the red buses. Here's a picture of Big Ben.

Can you come to my birthday party?

Love, Harry

Mrs Benson
5 Birch Street
Portsmouth
Hants PO12 2TB

Dear Mum,

London is great! I love it here!
This is our plan for today:
At 9 a.m. we are going to Tower Bridge. It's a big bridge.
At 12.15 p.m. we are having lunch at a sandwich bar. At 2.30 p.m. we are going to Hyde Park to play football and eat ice cream.

See you on the weekend.
Love, Kate

Mrs William
12 Morgan Street
Band

Look at Kate's text message. What does she write?

1 Read the dialogues.

2 Act out the dialogues.

★ Make up your own dialogue.

Story: The Earl of Sandwich

Note

Who was the Earl of Sandwich?
Find out more about him on the Internet.

S8 L22 **1** Listen to the story.

2 Read the dialogue with a partner. Listen and point.

3 Act it out.

Note

In what other countries are there still kings or queens?
Make a list.
Think. Pair. Share.

1 **Listen. Point to the pictures.** L26

2 **Read the sentences.**

People in Britain love the Royal Family.

Royal guards are in front of Buckingham Palace.

The Royals are everywhere.

3 **Read the sentences. Find the right pictures.**

4 **Talk about activities and times. Say:** ***At 10 a.m., William ...***

Note

a.m. = in the morning
p.m. = in the afternoon

One day in the life of two Royals.

08:00 a.m.	Kate takes her dog for a walk.
10:00 a.m.	William visits a football team.
12:00 p.m.	Kate and William have lunch.
02:00 p.m.	Kate visits pupils at a London school.
07:30 p.m.	Kate and William are at a concert.

All year round

1 Talk about the picture.

There's/There are .../I can see .../It's cold and cloudy/...

2 Read the sentences.

Note

cloud – cloud**y**
sun – sunn**y**
wind – ...
Find out more!

Let's talk

1 Read the dialogue. Talk to a partner.

☆ More: Make up your own dialogue.

2 Look at the pictures. Talk to a partner.

In Rome it's …

1

Rome (19° C)

2

New York (3° C)

3

4

Paris (23° C)

5

Ankara (33° C)

6

London (13° C)

Note

What is the weather like today in Rome, Paris, …? Find out!

My birthday is in spring.

1 Read and match.

Hi, I'm Robin.
My birthday is in September, in autumn. In autumn, the leaves turn red and yellow. When it is windy, I like flying my kite. Do you like my birthday cake?

Hello, my name is Oona.
I was born in summer, in July. When it is sunny and hot, I like eating ice cream. What do you do in summer?

Hi, I'm Arian.
My birthday is in April, in spring. In spring, there are lots of flowers. I like looking for Easter eggs. Do you like my tree?

Hello, my name is Mathilda. My birthday is in winter, in February. Sometimes it is cold and snowy on my birthday. I like playing in the snow. Do you like my snowman?

2 Answer the questions.

- When is Robin's/… birthday? Say: *Robin's birthday is in …*
- What's the weather like in spring/…? Say: *In spring it's …*
- What do the children like? Say: *Robin likes …*
- What about you? Say: *My birthday is in …*

1 Talk about the pictures. Is the weather normal or extreme?

2 Read the texts. Match the texts (A-D) with the pictures.

A Hi, I'm Mark. I live in Australia. We often have extreme weather in our country. Look at this big bushfire near Sydney! A lot of animals and trees died and people lost their homes.

B Hi, I'm Elaine. I live in Florida, USA. From June until November we often have hurricanes. They destroy houses, trees and fields. There's a lot of rain and some animals and people die.

C Hello, I'm Oscar. I live in Zimbabwe, Africa. It's always very hot, sunny and dry here. There's no rain, so the plants don't grow well. We are often hungry.

D Hi, my name is Emma. I live in Germany. We had so much rain! Now there's too much water in the river. We have to go to school by boat! Look – all the streets, houses and gardens are flooded.

★ What extreme weather do you sometimes see in Germany?

3 How can YOU help to reduce extreme weather events?

Think. Pair. Share.

→ DVD 1 Fächerübergreifendes Lernen: „Science", s. HRU, S. 287–288

What I can do and say

A word web

food and shopping

bread
butter
cheese
chicken
egg
ham
salad
tea
tomato
water

apple · chocolate
fruit · sweets

How many ...?   to eat/drink

Hi, can I help you?
Can I have a/an/ some ..., please?
I'd like ...
How much is it?
It's ...
Here you are.
Enjoy your meal.
Thank you.
...

Make your own word web

Think. Pair. Share.

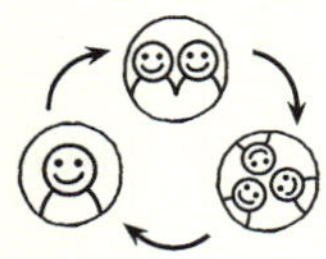

time

school

birthdays

When is (your birthday)? · My birthday is in .../It's in ... · Happy birthday! · I like (sports) .../I don't like ... · I have English at 9:30. · I like German/English/P.E./... · My favourite subject is ... · My teacher is ... · Excuse me, please. What time is it? – It's ...

What can you do or say in English? Think!

I can ... ... say the words.
... write the words.
... ask and answer questions.

What do you want to be better at?

What I can do and say

How to talk about pictures:

You don't know the word in English?

Ask your teacher or partner.

Mime!

Play 'mime and guess'.

At the museum

In the museum there's/there are …

1 What animals are in the museum?

2 Read the speech bubbles. Talk to a partner.

★ Can you find the Natural History Museum on the London map? (Look at page 6/7.)

Note

Do research:
What can you find out about the Natural History Museum (for example: opening hours, prices, animals, special events)?

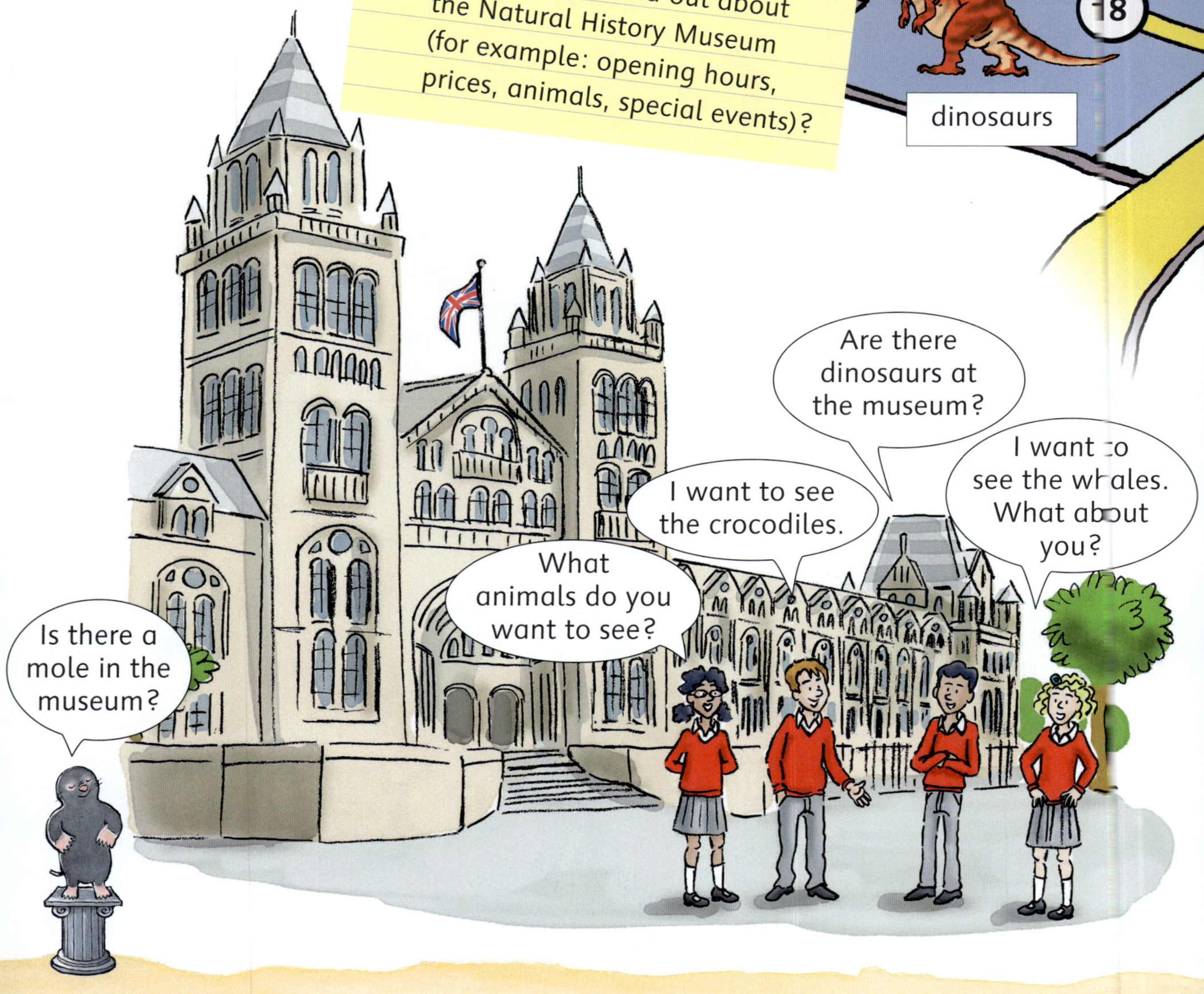

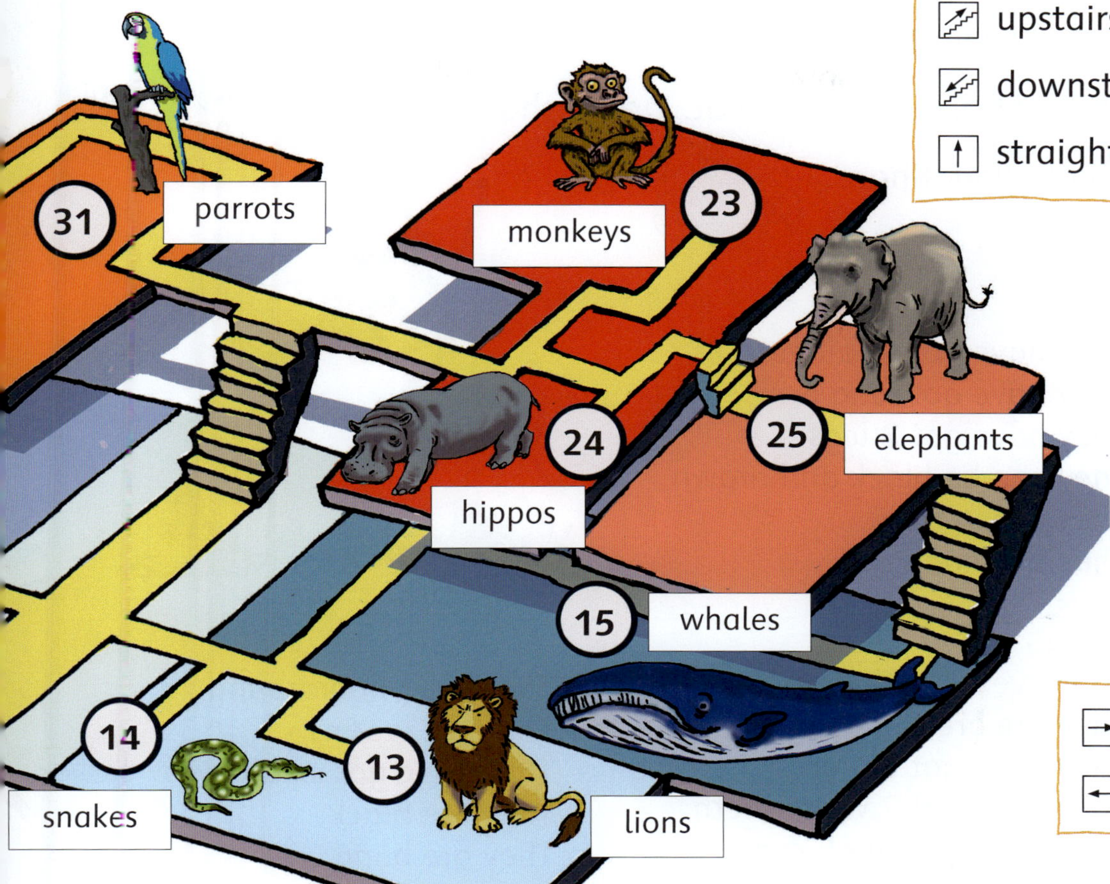

upstairs
downstairs
straight ahead

right
left

Let's talk

3 Read the dialogue. Talk to a partner.

☆ More: Make up your own dialogue.

1 Listen to your partner. Say the word for the animal.

2 Think of one more animal. Draw, show and talk.

My animal has got …

Think. Pair. Share.

They have got small ears.
They have got long arms.
They have got 2 legs.
They can be black and brown.
They live in trees.
They like bananas.

They live in the jungle.
They are grey.
They have got big ears.
They have got 2 white teeth.
They have got small eyes.
They have got big legs.

They live underground.
They eat worms.
They have got small eyes.
They are black.
They are blind.

Read the presentation rules.

Make notes.

Know your text.

Speak loudly.

Look at the class.

Show pictures.

1 Talk about the pictures.

2 Read the speech bubbles.

3 Complete the speech bubbles. Work with a partner.

1 Listen. Point to the pictures. (L 40)

2 Read the texts.

The Jurassic Coast is a region in South England.

1 Jurassic Coast

2 dinosaur fossil

3 dinosaur footprint

4 ammonites

5 a fish

6 dinosaur museum

Note

At the Dinosaur museum in Dorchester you can learn a lot about dinosaurs.
What was the biggest, smallest, longest, fastest or heaviest dinosaur?
Find out!
Think. Pair. Share.

→ DVD 3

Keeping fit

1 Talk about the picture.

There's/
There are .../
I can see ...

Note
I cannot = I can't

L46 **1** Listen. What can Linda do?

2 Read the dialogue with a partner.

Make up your own dialogue. Think. Pair. Share.

Note
Record your interview.

1 Listen. Point to the pictures.

2 Read the story.

① 

Mia loves basketball.
Mia loves baseball.
But most of all, Mia loves soccer.
She plays every day with her brothers and sisters.

Sometimes the ball sails to the left of the net. Or to the right.
Or her sister, the goalie, saves the ball with her hands.
No goal. No cheering.

 ②

③ 

'I quit!'
'Sorry, Mia. Quitters can't play on my team.
If you can't learn to lose you can't play.'

Maybe she can score the goal.
Maybe she can't.
But she is playing.
Playing is more important than winning or losing …

 ④

⑤ 

… because winners never quit!

Note

Find out more about the author Mia Hamm on the Internet.

1 Listen and point to the pictures.

L 49

1 
2 
3 
4 

Note

Viele englische Kinder spielen *rounders* auf dem Schulhof. Kennst du ein ähnliches Spiel?

2 Look at the pictures. Read the rules.

Explain the rules.

You need:

 a bat	 a ball	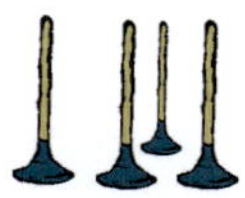 4 posts	 6-15 players

(1) Form two teams.

batting team

fielding team

(2) Choose a bowler.

bowler

(3) The bowler bowls the ball.
The batter hits the ball.

(4) The batter runs from post to post.

The team with the most rounders wins.

Fächerübergreifendes Lernen: „Sports", s. HRU, S. 289–292

→ DVD 4

Emails from the USA

Note

Dein Name, deine Adresse, deine Telefonnummer oder dein Geburtsdatum gehen nicht jeden etwas an. Sprich immer zuerst mit deiner Lehrerin, deinem Lehrer oder deinen Eltern, bevor du im Internet von dir erzählst.

1 Talk about the picture.

2 Read and answer the questions.

1 Talk about the pictures.

Note

Americans pay with dollars ($) and cents.
How much is 1 € in $?
Find out on the Internet.

1 Statue of Liberty

2 Empire State Building

3 Central Park

4 Brooklyn Bridge

5 yellow cab

S15 L51

2 Listen to Matt's rap. Point to the pictures.

3 Read the text.

★ Do the rap.

Welcome to New York!
Welcome to the sights!
Welcome to the city
that never sleeps at night.

Go to Central Park,
have a picnic in the sun.
Skate, skate, play or walk,
have lots of fun.

New York City is the place 2 B. Yo!
New York City is the place 4 me.

The Empire State Building
is very high.
One hundred an' three
floors up to the sky.

Over Brooklyn Bridge
you can bike, walk or ride.
Or take a yellow cab
from side to side.

One more sight
you have to see
and that's the famous
Statue of Liberty.

1 Read Kate's email. What does she write about?

New message

To mattman@example.com

Subject About my family

Dear Matt,
Today I want to write about my family. I live with my mum and dad.
Where do you live? Do you have a big family?
My dad has got a second-hand shop. My mum is a hairdresser.
I've got a sister. She's older than me. She's a shop assistant. I haven't got a brother, but I've got a lot of friends.
My best friends are Harry, Samir and Emily. We like playing in Harry's garden and in the street. I don't like playing soccer and I hate computer games. What do you like doing?
My grandmother lives in London. I love London. There's so much to see there. I went there in September with Harry and my dad.

What's your family like?

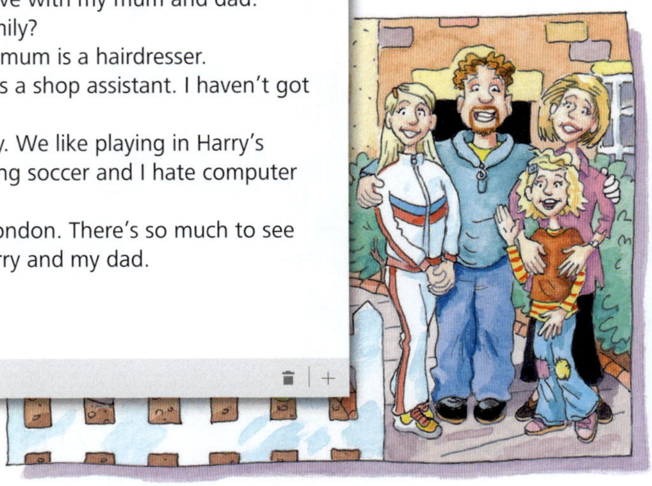

Note

What media do you use to contact your friends?

L55 2 Listen to Matt's email.

3 Read the text.

New message

To kitty@example.com

Subject About me

Hi Kate,
Thanks for your email. I'm ten years old.
My birthday is in November.
I've got a brother. He's a mechanic. And I've got a little sister. My mother is a teacher. My father works in the city. He's a taxi driver. I've got two hamsters.
I like playing with my hamsters.
My hobbies are playing computer games and reading.
What are your hobbies?

Your friend,
Matt

Send

Note

What is your mother's and your father's job? Look in a dictionary.

Story: A day in New York

1 Talk about the pictures.

2 Listen to your teacher.
Point to the speech bubbles.

Read the story.

→ DVD 5

1 Read the texts about John, the police officer.

2 Listen to your partner. Point to the right picture.

Hello, my name is John.
I'm a police officer
in New York City.

In the city
we go by car.

You can go
very fast on a motorbike.

In Central Park
we ride horses.

I can see more
from a helicopter.

Do you like my badge?

L59 **2** Listen. Talk to a partner.

More: Make up your own dialogue.

What I can do and say

A word web

sports and hobbies

play football ride a bike/horse skateboard ski snowboard sports swim tennis

I play table tennis.
He/She plays …

What's your hobby? Do you like/love/hate …? I like/love/hate … I don't like/love/hate …

dance · do judo/ballet   Have you got a …? Yes, I have. It's …

Make your own word web

Think. Pair. Share.

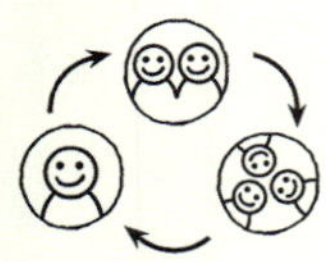

feelings

family

This is/These are my … · Have you got a …?–Yes, I've got …/No, I haven't got … · He/She has got … · How many … have you got? · What's his/her name?–His/Her name is … · How old is he/she?–He's/She's … · He/She lives in … · How are you?–I'm happy/sad/OK/okay. · I'm cold/hot. · How do you feel?–I feel …

What can you do or say in English? Think!

I can … … say the words.
… write the words.
… ask and answer questions.

What do you want to be better at?

What I can do and say

How to present:

Think. Make notes.

Look at your notes.
Use pictures.
Speak slowly.

Team game: 'Whispering chain'.

You need:
One set of picture cards.

1) Listen to your teacher.

2) Whisper the word to the next pupil in line.

3) Find the matching card.
Show it to your teacher.
Is it the right card?
Well done!
One point for you.

Looking back at Sunshine

1 What did you learn?
What can you say in English?
Read the texts.

2 Talk about the units.

Think. Pair. Share.

I know the colours and numbers in English

I can talk about my family and friends.

I can say which pets I like.

How did

I can talk about my school things.

That was OK.

That was not so good.

That was great!

I can talk about clothes.

class 3

I can talk about rooms and furniture.

I can read a story book.

I can buy food and drinks.

class 4

I can say what time it is.

I can talk about the weather, seasons and my birthday month.

I can do a presentation about animals.

Know your text.

Speak loudly.

Look at the class.

Show pictures.

I can say what my hobbies are.

I can read the story about Mia, the soccer player.

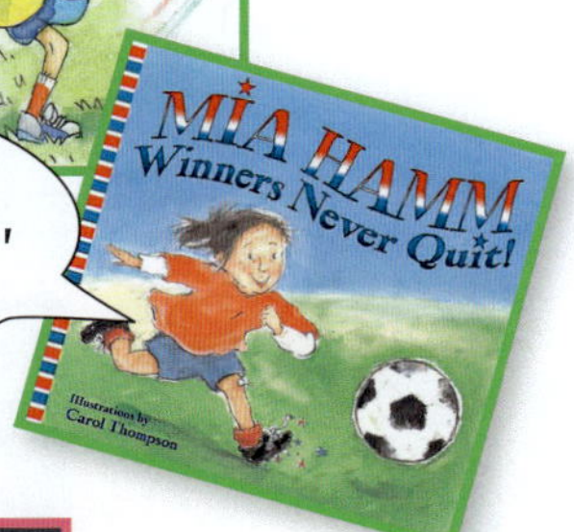

I can write about myself and my family.

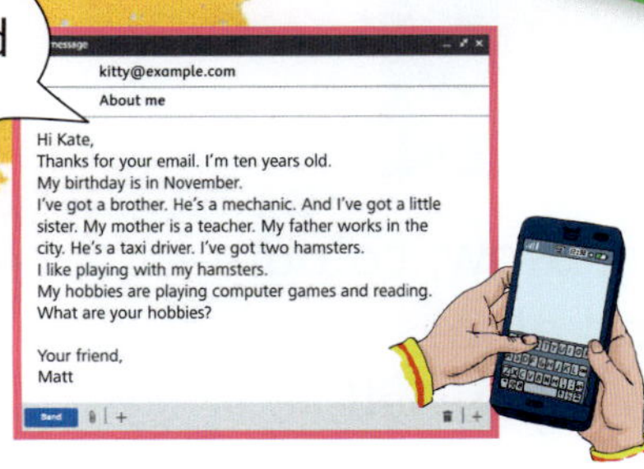

I know about Halloween.

you like it?

I like/love/hate ...

I don't like/love/hate ... because ...

My favourite words are ...

I was good at ...

I want to learn more about ...

6 Making a lapbook

You need:

- photocopies (KV 51-58)
- a coloured piece of cardboard paper (DIN A3)
- a piece of paper (DIN A4) in a different colour
- your pencil case, scissors and a glue stick

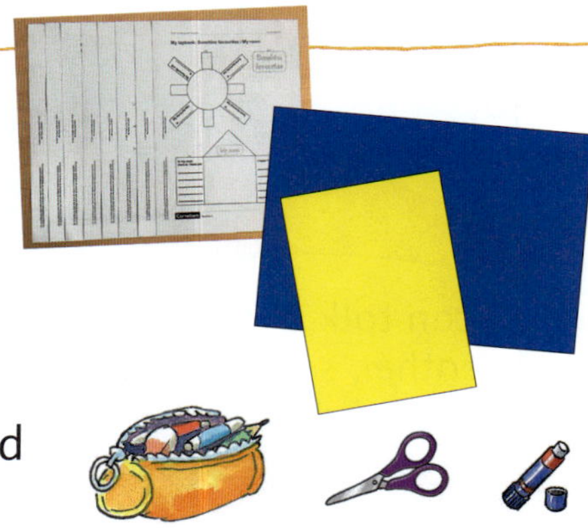

Now you can start:

1. Fold your cardboard paper from each side to the centre.

2. Glue your coloured paper into the centre of your lapbook.

3. Now write, draw, colour in, cut out and glue:
   Write about yourself.
   What about your family?
   Design your room.

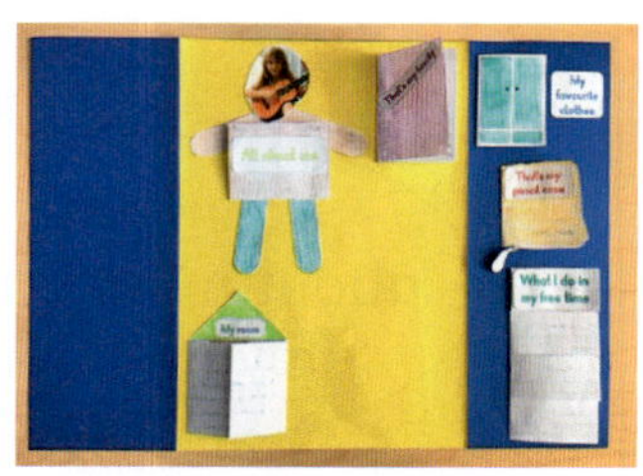

4. Put your clothes in the wardrobe.
   Draw what is in your pencil case.
   What do you do in your free time?

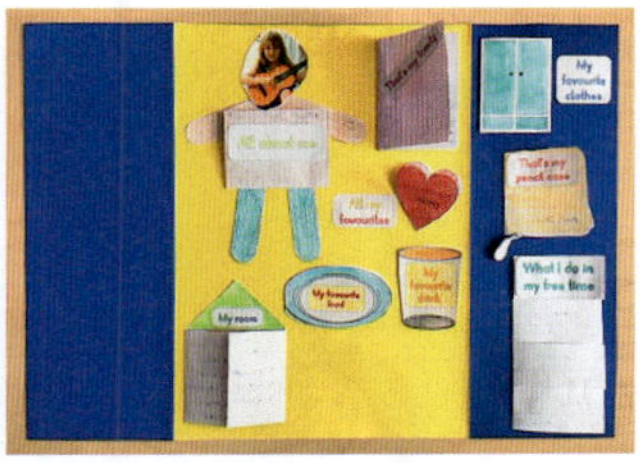

5) What is your favourite food and your favourite drink? What are your favourites?

6) Cut out the moles.
Draw or write about the animals you like.
Write the words you like.

7) Write the countries you know. Colour in the flags. What are your Sunshine favourites? Think about it and write.

8) Design your cover.
Choose the pictures you like.

9) You are finished – great job!

Now you can present your lapbook to the class.

Note

Hast du schon mal eine richtige Schulinspektion erlebt? Vergleiche!

S 18 L 60 **1** Listen.
Point to the pictures.

2 Read the story.

6
Do you know a rhyme?
Of course, we do!
I can say: The elephant goes like this and that.
7
Can you read?
Of course, we can!
I know a story about the Earl of Sandwich.
8
That was bad!
No, that isn't right, Inspector.
9
I'm not the school inspector. I'm the new caretaker!
He's the new caretaker!
He isn't the school inspector!
10
11
That was a very good lesson, Mrs Brown!
Thank you, Ms Honey. They're good pupils.

1 Talk about the picture.

How many ghosts, monsters, pumpkins, skeletons, ... are there?

S19 L74 2 Listen to the rhyme.

3 Say the rhyme.

Special days: Bonfire Night

1 Talk about the pictures.

S20 L75 2 Listen to the rhyme.

Read the rhyme.

Say the rhyme.

Remember, remember
the fifth of November,
gunpowder, treason and plot.
I see no reason
why gunpowder treason
should ever be forgot.

Special days: Christmas

S21 L77 **1** Listen to the story. Point to the pictures.

Read the story.

Sing the song. Find the matching pictures.

Rudolph is a reindeer. He has a red nose.

The other reindeer laugh at Rudolph's nose.

Poor Rudolph is sad.

It is Christmas Eve. It is very foggy. Santa asks Rudolph for help.

Rudolph helps Santa.

Rudolph is very happy. The reindeer are his friends now.

So verändern sich die Wörter in der Mehrzahl:
Wenn du von mehreren Dingen sprichst, hängst du ein ‚s' an.

one book – two book**s,** one apple – two apple**s**

➜ Es gibt Ausnahmen, die du dir merken musst:

one child – two child**ren**
one hobb**y** – two hobb**ies**
one reindeer – two reindeer

So sagst du, dass jemanden etwas gehört:

This is Tim**'s** book.

This is Anne**'s** pencil case.

Finde Beispiele in deinem Pupil's Book!

Diese Wörter brauchst du, um Fragen zu stellen:

What? = Was?
What is this? Was ist das?

When? = Wann?
When is your birthday?

Where? = Wo?
Where is my book?

Who? = Wer?
Who is on the phone?

How? = Wie?
How are you?

How many? = Wie viele?
How many children like chocolate?

How much? = Wie viel?
How much is the orange juice?

➜ Es gibt Ausnahmen, die du dir merken musst:

How much is …? = Was kostet …?
What time is it? = Wie spät ist es?
What's your name? = Wie heißt du?

So fangen viele Fragen an:

Do you like …? = Magst du …?
Can I have …? = Kann ich … haben?
Have you got …? = Hast du …?
Are you happy/sad/angry? = Bist du glücklich, traurig, wütend?

Looking at English

So kannst du über dich und andere sprechen:

I am

you are

he is

she is

it is

we are

you are

they are

Manche Wörter werden abgekürzt: I am = I'm

I am = I'm
you are = you're
he is = he's
she is = she's
it is = it's
we are = we're
you are = you're
they are = they're

I am verwendest du, wenn du etwas aufschreibst, **I'm** verwendest du, wenn du etwas sagst.

I cannot = I can't
where is = where's
what is = what's

I would like = I'd like
I have got = I've got

Finde Beispiele in deinem Pupil's Book!

Manche Wörter haben mehrere Bedeutungen:

it · the · you

it = es*
the = der, die, das
you = du, ihr

* (Das Wort 'it' bedeutet 'es', steht aber auch für 'er' oder 'sie' bei Nomen, die im Deutschen männlich oder weiblich sind, z. B. 'the moon – it' oder 'the sun – it'.)

A
about über
afternoon Nachmittag
again noch einmal, wieder
angry verärgert
animal Tier
answer antworten, Lösung
Art Kunst (Schulfach)
ask fragen
at bei, im, um
autumn Herbst

B
back Rücken
bad schlecht
ballet Ballett
basketball Basketball
be sein
because weil
behind hinter
belly Bauch
bend beugen
big groß
bill Rechnung
birthday Geburtstag
blackboard Tafel
blow out auspusten
boat Boot
bonfire Lagerfeuer
book Buch
boy Junge
bread Brot
breakfast Frühstück
brother Bruder
bus Bus
bus driver Busfahrer/in
bush Busch
but aber
butter Butter
buy kaufen

C
calendar Kalender
camel Kamel
can können
candle Kerze
car Auto
caretaker Hausmeister
chair Stuhl
cent (hier: amerikanischer) Cent
cheese Käse
chicken Huhn
chips Pommes frites
chocolate Schokolade
Christmas Weihnachten
city Großstadt
clap klatschen
class Klasse
classroom Klassenraum
clock Uhr
clock tower Glockenturm
cloudy wolkig
club AG, Klub, Verein
colour Farbe, ausmalen
come kommen
Computers Computer (Schulfach)
crocodile Krokodil
cut out ausschneiden

D
daffodil Osterglocke
dance tanzen
dangerous gefährlich
day Tag
Dear … Liebe/r …
degree(s) Grad
dinner Abendessen
dinosaur Dinosaurier
do machen, tun
do ballet Ballett tanzen
do judo Judo betreiben
dollar ($) (hier: amerikanischer) Dollar
door Tür
downstairs unten
draw zeichnen
dream Traum
drink trinken, Getränk
driver Fahrer

E
ear Ohr
eat essen
egg Ei
elephant Elefant
email E-Mail
England England
English englisch, Englisch (Schulfach)
Enjoy your meal! Guten Appetit!
e-pal E-Mail-Freund/in
euro (€) Euro
evening Abend
eye Auge

F
famous berühmt
father Vater
Father Christmas Weihnachtsmann
favourite Lieblings-
feed füttern
fireworks Feuerwerk
flag Flagge
flap auf und ab bewegen
fly fliegen
foggy neblig

food Essen
foot, feet Fuß, Füße
football Fußball
forget vergessen
forward vorwärts
Friday Freitag
from aus, von

G

game Spiel
German deutsch, Deutsch (Schulfach)
Germany Deutschland
ghost Geist
giraffe Giraffe
girl Mädchen
give geben
glue kleben
go gehen
Good luck! Viel Glück!
Goodness gracious! Du meine Güte!
grandfather, grandpa Großvater, Opa
grandmother, grandma Großmutter, Oma
Great Britain Großbritannien
gunpowder Schießpulver

H

hairdresser Friseur/in
half past halb (Uhrzeit)
Halloween Halloween
ham Schinken
happen geschehen
happy glücklich
hate hassen
have (got) haben
have to müssen
he er
head Kopf
hello hallo
help helfen, Hilfe
helpful hilfreich
her ihr/ihre
here hier
hippo Nilpferd
his sein/seine
hobby Hobby
holidays Ferien
(at) home zu Hause
hop hopsen, springen
hope hoffen
horse Pferd
hot heiß, warm
house Haus
how wie
how many wie viele
how much wie viel

I

idea Idee
ill krank
in in
in front of vor
inspector Inspektor/in, Schulrat/-rätin
is ist
it es

J

job Beruf, Job
judo Judo
jump springen
jungle Dschungel

K

king König
kite Drachen
knee Knie
know kennen, wissen

L

late spät
leaf, leaves Blatt, Blätter
left links
leg Bein
lesson Schulstunde
Let's go! Los!
lettuce Kopfsalat
line Linie, Reihe
lion Löwe
listening to music Musik hören
little klein
live leben, wohnen
long lang
look at betrachten
loud, loudly laut
love lieben
Love, ... Liebe Grüße ...
lunch Mittagessen

M

make machen
many viel/e
matches Streichhölzer
Maths Mathe (Schulfach)
mechanic Mechaniker/in
meeting friends Freunde treffen
miss a turn aussetzen
Monday Montag
monkey Affe
morning Morgen
mother Mutter

motorbike Motorrad
move (sich) bewegen
much viel
museum Museum
Music Musik (Schulfach)
my mein/e

N

name Name
next to neben
nice nett
nickname Spitzname
nose Nase
not nicht
notes Noten, Notizen
number Nummer

O

o'clock ...Uhr
of course natürlich
old alt
on auf
open offen/öffnen

P

P.E. (= Physical Education) Sport (Schulfach)
paper Papier
parrot Papagei
pass (sth.) (etwas) reichen
password Passwort
photo Foto
picture Bild
plane Flugzeug
play spielen, Theaterspiel
please bitte
plot Verschwörung
point to auf ... zeigen
police officer Polizist/in
police station Polizeiwache
postcard Postkarte
present Geschenk
pumpkin Kürbis
pupil Schüler/in
put legen, stellen

Q

quarter past/to viertel nach/vor (Uhrzeit)
queen Königin
quiet leise

R

rainy regnerisch
read lesen
remember erinnern
rhyme Reim
ride a horse reiten
right rechts
river Fluss
rose Rose
run laufen

S

sad traurig
salad (zubereiteter) Salat
Santa, Santa Claus Weihnachtsmann (in den USA)
Saturday Samstag
savannah Savanne
say sagen
scared verängstigt
Science Sachunterricht (Schulfach)
sea Meer
season Jahreszeit
see sehen
she sie
shop assistant Verkäufer/in
short kurz
shoulder Schulter
show zeigen
sight Sehenswürdigkeit
sing singen
sister Schwester
sit sitzen
skeleton Skelett
ski Ski, Ski fahren
small klein
snake Schlange
snap schnipsen
snowdrop Schneeglöckchen
snowy verschneit
speak sprechen
spider Spinne
sports Sportarten
spring Frühling
stamp aufstampfen
star Star
straight ahead geradeaus
street Straße
stretch dehnen, strecken
strong stark
subject Fach, Schulfach
summer Sommer
Sunday Sonntag
sunny sonnig
sweets Süßigkeiten
swim schwimmen

T

table Tisch
table tennis Tischtennis
tail Schwanz
talk reden
taxi Taxi
taxi driver Taxifahrer/in

tea Tee
teacher Lehrer/in
temperature Temperatur
tennis Tennis
text message, SMS SMS
there dort
they sie
this diese/r/s
throw werfen
Thursday Donnerstag
ticket Fahrkarte
tiger Tiger
time Zeit
timetable Stundenplan
to nach, zu
today heute
toe Zeh
toilet Toilette
tomato/es Tomate/n
tooth, teeth Zahn, Zähne
touch anfassen, berühren
train Zug
treason Verrat
tree Baum
Tuesday Dienstag
tummy Bauch
turn abbiegen
turn around umdrehen

U

under unter
underground U-Bahn
understand verstehen
upstairs oben
USA USA (= Vereinigte Staaten von Amerika)
useful nützlich

V

Vampire Vampir

W

walk gehen
want wollen
watching TV fernsehen
water Wasser
we wir
weather Wetter
weather report Wetterbericht
Wednesday Mittwoch
weekend Wochenende
welcome willkommen
whale Wal
what was
wheel Rad
when wann
where wo
who wer
why warum
wiggle hin und her bewegen, zappeln
wild wild
windy windig
winter Winter
wish wünschen
witch Hexe

A

abbiegen turn
Abend evening
Abendessen dinner
Affe monkey
alt old
anfassen touch
anschauen look at
antworten answer
auf on
auf und ab bewegen flap
aufstampfen stamp
auf ... zeigen point to
Auge eye
aus from
ausmalen colour (in)
ausschneiden cut out
aussetzen miss a turn
Auto car

B

Ballett ballet
Ballett machen do ballet
Basketball basketball
Bauch belly, tummy
Baum tree
bei at
Bein leg
Beruf job
berühmt famous
berühren touch
beugen bend
(sich) bewegen move
Bild picture
bitte please
Blatt, Blätter leaf, leaves
Boot boat
Brot bread
Bruder brother
Buch book
Bus bus
Busch bush
Busfahrer/in bus driver
Butter butter

C

Cent cent
Computer (Schulfach) Computers

D

dehnen stretch
Deutsch (Schulfach), deutsch German
Deutschland Germany
Dienstag Tuesday
diese/r/s this
Dinosaurier dinosaur
Dollar ($) dollar
Donnerstag Thursday
dort there
Drachen kite
Dschungel jungle
Du meine Güte! Goodness gracious!

E

Ei egg
Elefant elephant
E-Mail email
E-Mail-Freund/in e-pal
England England
Englisch (Schulfach), englisch English
er he
erinnern remember
es it
essen eat
Essen food
Euro (€) euro

F

Fach, Schulfach subject
Fahrer driver
Fahrkarte ticket
Farbe colour
Ferien holidays
fernsehen watching TV
Feuerwerk fireworks
Flagge flag
fliegen fly
Flugzeug plane
Fluss river
Foto photo
fragen ask
Freitag Friday
Freunde treffen meeting friends
Friseur/in hairdresser
Frühling spring
Frühstück breakfast
Fuß, Füße foot, feet
Fußball football
füttern feed

G

geben give
gefährlich dangerous
gehen go, walk
Geist ghost
geradeaus straight ahead
geschehen happen
Geschenk present
Getränk drink
Giraffe giraffe
Glockenturm clock tower
glücklich happy
Grad degree(s)
groß big
Großbritannien Great Britain

Großmutter grandmother
Großstadt city
Großvater grandfather
Guten Appetit! Enjoy your meal!

H

haben have (got)
halb (Uhrzeit) half past/to
hallo hello
Halloween Halloween
hassen hate
Haus house
Hausmeister caretaker
heiß hot
helfen help
Herbst autumn
heute today
Hexe witch
hier here
hin und her bewegen, zappeln wiggle
Hilfe help
hilfreich helpful
Hobby hobby
hoffen hope
hopsen hop
Huhn chicken

I

Idee idea
ihr, ihre her, its
in in
ist is

J

Jahreszeit season
Job job
Judo judo
Judo betreiben do judo

K

Kalender calendar
Kamel camel
Käse cheese
kaufen buy
kennen know
Klasse class
Klassenraum classroom
klatschen clap
kleben glue
Klebstift glue stick
Kleid dress
klein little, small
Klub, AG club
Knie knee
kommen come
König king
Königin queen
können can
Kopf head
Kopfsalat lettuce
krank ill
Krokodil crocodile
Kunst (Schulfach) Art
Kürbis pumpkin
kurz short

L

Lagerfeuer bonfire
lang long
laufen run
laut loud, loudly
leben, wohnen live
legen put
Lehrer/in teacher
leise quiet
lesen read
Liebe/r ... Dear ...
Liebe Grüße ... Love, ...
lieben love
Lieblings- favourite
Linie line
links left
Los! Let's go!
Löwe lion

M

machen do, make
Mathe (Schulfach) Maths
Mechaniker/in mechanic
Meer sea
mein/e my
Mittagessen lunch
Mittwoch Wednesday
Montag Monday
Morgen morning
Motorrad motorbike
Museum museum
Musik (Schulfach) Music
Musik hören listening to music
müssen have to
Mutter mother

N

nach, zu to
Nachmittag afternoon
Name name
Nase nose
natürlich of course
neben next to
neblig foggy
nett nice
nicht not
Nilpferd hippo
noch einmal again
Noten, Notizen notes
Nummer number
nützlich useful

O

oben upstairs
offen open
Ohr ear
Oma grandma
Opa grandpa
Osterglocke daffodil

P

Papagei parrot
Papier paper
Passwort password
Pferd horse
Polizeiwache police station
Polizist/in police officer
Pommes frites chips
Postkarte postcard

R

Rad wheel
Rechnung bill
rechts right
reden talk
regnerisch rainy
(etwas) reichen pass (sth.)
Reihe line
Reim rhyme
reiten ride a horse
Rose rose
Rücken back

S

Sachunterricht (Schulfach) Science
sagen say
Salat (zubereitet) salad
Samstag Saturday
Savanne savannah
Schießpulver gunpowder
Schinken ham
Schlange snake
schlecht bad
Schneeglöckchen snowdrop
schnipsen snap
Schokolade chocolate
Schüler/in pupil
Schulfach (school) subject
Schulstunde lesson
Schulter shoulder
Schwanz tail
Schwester sister
schwimmen swim
sehen look, see
Sehenswürdigkeit sight
sein be
sein/e his
sein/e, ihr/e its
sie she, they
singen sing
sitzen sit
Skelett skeleton
Ski, Ski fahren ski
SMS SMS, text message
Sommer summer
sonnig sunny
Sonntag Sunday
spät late
Spiel game
spielen play
Spinne spider
Spitzname nickname
Sport (Schulfach) P.E. (= Physical Education)
Sportarten sports
sprechen speak
springen jump
Star star
stark strong
stellen put
Straße street
strecken stretch
Stuhl chair
Stundenplan timetable
Süßigkeiten sweets

T

Tafel blackboard
Tag day
tanzen dance
Taxi taxi
Taxifahrer/in taxi driver
Tee tea
Temperatur temperature
Tennis tennis
Theaterspiel play
Tier animal
Tiger tiger
Tisch table
Tischtennis table tennis
Toilette toilet
Tomate/n tomato/es
Traum dream
traurig sad
trinken drink
Tür door

U

U-Bahn underground
über about
Uhr clock, … o'clock
um at
umdrehen turn around
unten downstairs
unter under
USA (Vereinigte Staaten von Amerika) USA

V

Vampir vampire
Vater father
verängstigt scared
verärgert angry
vergessen forget
Verkäufer/in shop assistant
Verrat treason
verschneit snowy
Verschwörung plot
verstehen understand
viel much
viel/e many
Viel Glück! Good luck!
viertel vor/nach (Uhrzeit) quarter to/past
von from
vor in front of
vorwärts forward

W

Wal whale
wann when
warm hot
warum why
was what
Wasser water
Weihnachten Christmas
Weihnachtsmann Father Christmas, Santa Claus (USA)
weil because
wer who
werfen throw
Wetter weather
Wetterbericht weather report
wie how
wie viel how much
wie viele how many
wild wild
willkommen welcome
windig windy
Winter winter
wir we
wissen know
wo where
Wochenende weekend
wohnen live
wolkig cloudy
wollen want
wünschen wish

Z

Zahn, Zähne tooth, teeth
Zeh toe
zeichnen draw
zeigen show
Zeit time
zu to
Zug train
zu Hause (at) home